MW00414398

Be HAPPY
in Both Worlds

You *can* have a successful career
and a happy family

SARAH L. RUFFI

Be Happy in Both Worlds

Editing by Philip L. Ransom   philipransom.com
Cover artwork by David Anthony Hummer
Cover design by Mallory Stoltz

ISBN 9781699291535

Independently published

Printed by Kindle Publishing Direct

Dedication Page

Female attorneys sometimes believe they need to put their families on hold while they establish their careers.
This book is dedicated to all those women who are torn between spending time with their families and practicing law. The good news is you don't have to choose. You can design your life to be happy in both worlds.

Acknowledgments

Thank you —

To my husband, Dwight, for his unwavering belief in me, his encouragement to share my experiences, and patience on my path to finding the balance between our family and my career.

To my four beautiful sons, Tony, Mac, Nic, and Joey, without whom I would probably still be working 80 hours a week.

To all the exchange students, especially Jasper Breeuwsma, who became part of our family and opened our world.

To my editor, Phil Ransom, for guiding me, providing insight and clarity.

Be HAPPY in Both Worlds

You *can* have a successful career *and* a happy family

Table of Contents

Hi, I'm Sarah

(Your author's back-story)

For as long as I can remember, I wanted to own my own business. I just didn't know what it would be. It took a long time, but I eventually figured it out.

As a strange 10-year-old kid, bored one summer, I asked my dad if I could go to work with him at the factory he ran where they made raincoats and waders. He told me I could provided I taught myself how to type. With a little determination, I taught myself how to type on an old manual typewriter, using the book my mom used in high school. (I know, I am dating myself.)

I practiced and practiced until eventually, my dad invited me to come to work with him; my own desk would be just outside his office. I learned about the importance of paying attention to detail and professionalism. I answered the phones, overheard his end of his phone calls, greeted people when they entered the office, and listened to him talk with customers, employees, and sales representatives. I watched everything happening around me while I experienced my dad's working world.

With auto-correct typewriters and computers still waiting to be invented, I had to re-type any documents with three or more white-out or correction-tape corrections on a page. I learned how to make things happen and figure out problems. Despite my work, I did not receive a regular paycheck for all of those hours; I worked the entire summer for a raincoat of my choice.

Shortly after my high school graduation, my parents bought a manufacturing business. They didn't have any marketing pieces, so that summer before college, I helped Dad create them for their product lines.

Throughout my college years, I helped with the family business while maintaining other jobs to make money for college. During my final semester of college, Dad told me that while I didn't have to come to work with them, he had a job for me if I wanted it. He outlined my proposed responsibilities, should I accept his offer. Because he knew my capabilities, he offered me significantly more responsibility than someone who didn't know me would.

I didn't want to return to my hometown. But as I weighed my dad's job offer against every position for which I interviewed, none compared to my opportunity at home. So after graduation, I returned home to work in the family business as their Marketing Coordinator. We had a deal. I would work in the company for two years, go to graduate school, earn my M.B.A., and then move on to something else.

As Marketing Coordinator, I designed brochures, developed a newsletter, created costing spreadsheets, and helped build the dealer network. Because I shared an office with my dad, I witnessed the issues that came through his door. I'd only been there six months or so when I realized all the legal issues that a business owner encounters – every day.

I'm a tad bit stubborn, you might say. I didn't want to run to a lawyer with a business issue every time I turned around, so I decided to go to law school. After all, if other people could finish law school, so could I!!

I didn't say anything to my parents for a few months, thinking I might change my mind. But I didn't. I don't think Dad was very surprised when I told him; he was extremely proud! The next time Konrad, the company's lawyer, came to the office for a meeting, my dad proudly told him about my plans. Konrad responded that I needed to start law school that fall, and my first summer out, I would work for him. I thanked him for the offer, but let him know that I planned to work another year and a half, then get my master's degree. Then, if I was still interested, go to law school, which is exactly what I did. (Did I mention I'm a tad bit stubborn?)

I clerked for Konrad during both summers of law school. At the end of the second summer, Konrad offered me a job, which I accepted. Unlike most of my classmates, I started my third year of law school, knowing that I already had my first legal job when I graduated. It relieved the pressure of searching for that first "lawyer" job.

What a challenging and rewarding job that was! Similar to my Dad, Konrad knew my capabilities and gave me a lot of freedom as a new lawyer. He reviewed my work and my pre-bills. He provided some guidance, but he didn't truly show me the ropes.

I learned many things by observing others. The older male lawyers on the other end of the phone, and the other side of cases, all thought I was just a little girl that they could easily manipulate. From my perspective, they believed that as long as they took a bold, brash attitude, voice, and posture, they would get what they wanted because I would give in to their demands. Boy, were they wrong! After practicing for two years, I became a partner in the firm.

Things went well at first. Not having a man in my life, I worked crazy-long hours and poured myself into my work. Shortly before I became a partner in the firm, I met Dwight. After dating a little over two years, we married and began our family. When our first son, Tony, was born, I took two months off for maternity leave. During those months, however, I billed more than enough hours to cover my salary. That didn't make my husband happy, but it was what I felt I had to do. We even have pictures of me holding Tony on one shoulder with a file open in front of me and the phone on my other shoulder! Talk about no work-life balance.

I was torn between my job and wanting to spend time with my new family when I returned to work. I scaled back the number of hours I worked, which did not make my partners happy. Nine months later, we learned there was another bundle of joy on the way. During my pregnancy, we had no indications of the challenges that awaited us.

Three hours after our second son, Mac, was born, the nurse discovered his blood oxygen level was dropping. She called the lead nurse, who in turn called the pediatrician on call. The pediatrician didn't know the cause of Mac's issues, so she called another hospital. That hospital sent a helicopter to get our son. Only four hours old, Mac was airlifted to the hospital an hour away from our home. As the flight crew took Mac into the helicopter, my doctor discharged me so Dwight and I could follow our new son, only to learn that the next doctor determined two hours later that he needed to be airlifted to Children's Hospital in Milwaukee!

The next morning, Dwight and I said goodbye to Tony, who was staying with my parents, and drove to Milwaukee. That three-hour trip seemed like an eternity. When we finally arrived, our son's doctor took us into a private room and explained the issue. Mac had transposition of the greater arteries. In English, that meant the arteries at the top of his heart were flipped. He wasn't getting oxygenated blood through his system because it kept cycling through his heart and lungs while the "dirty" blood kept cycling through the rest of his little body. If he had been born ten years earlier, he wouldn't have survived. Thank God for advances in medicine!

Fortunately, Children's had the top two neonatal neurosurgeons in the country at the time, and they were able to correct little six-day-old Mac's condition surgically. Dwight and I barely left Mac's side while he was at Children's. He was the hospital's star patient and was released to go home five days after surgery. I probably don't need to tell you that my family was first on my mind and my practice was last at that point. I didn't want to go to work, though I loved my clients. I wanted to be with Mac, Tony, and Dwight.

I actually took two full months off for maternity leave and returned to work around Thanksgiving. My second maternity leave was in sharp contrast to the first. I didn't worry about any files. I took care of my baby.

When I returned to work, I noticed that my partners were watching my every move. They looked at the clock when I came to work. They looked at the clock when I left work. They paid attention to what I did and where I went. Essentially, they watched everything about my work life. I didn't like or appreciate it.

I unknowingly took my work issues home with me in my mind, which compounded the tensions there. I did not take my frustrations out on my partners or confront them. Instead, continually stressed, I took my frustrations out on my young family. I had a very short temper and exploded at Dwight over little things. It got bad. Really bad. Nobody in my house was happy, except maybe Mac, who was only a couple months old.

By early December, life at home was unbearable. One night, Dwight gave me the ultimatum that I either left the firm or we would be divorced. I learned he had his escape with the boys all planned, should I choose the firm over them. Well, it wasn't a difficult choice! I loved my husband and sons way more than my partners. But it scared me, because Dwight stayed home with our sons, and I supported the family!

Shortly after my husband's ultimatum, we had our end of the year shareholder meeting at the firm to discuss how to divide up the year's profits. The meeting began with one of my partners telling me that I wasn't working hard enough, wasn't billing enough, wasn't out in the community enough and nobody knew me. Great. Just what I needed to hear.

That night, my husband woke up at 2:00 a.m. to me crying in bed. He asked me what was wrong and I told him that I didn't want to go to work.

"Then don't," he said. To him, it was simple. To me, it wasn't. I believed that I had to go to work because I was the sole source of income for our young family. But we began to plan my escape from the firm.

We put a plan together with the goal of me opening my own firm in July, seven months later. My partners had changed the compensation structure, and I was expecting a big bonus at the end of June. It would be perfect. My husband had a gut feeling and kept telling me, "We don't have that much time."

I didn't believe him.

I moved the target date to April. Again, he told me, "You don't have that much time." With two little boys in tow, my husband began looking for office space. It felt like we were in a race to beat the clock. I wanted to be able to walk out of my old firm and into a new firm, prepared to open for business! Little did I know, we were in a race to beat the clock of when my partners would learn of my plan.

One day in January, talking to a client, who also happened to be my banker, I confidentially asked him how much it would take to open a law firm and if I could borrow the money from his bank. I told him that I needed to keep it strictly confidential because if my partners found out, I would be out of a job. During our conversation, he suggested that I call another local attorney, Buster, who had semi-retired by closing his office and moving to a different firm. The banker believed that his office space was still available. Dwight called Buster and looked at the space. It was available and perfect for us.

We began to tag-team. I worked during the day, and Dwight watched the boys. At night and on weekends, Dwight worked on getting our new office ready while I watched the boys. We decided that I would give my partners notice of my intention to leave in mid-March and be out by the end of March.

And then February 19th happened. My partners learned about my plans. On my way to the office, on Friday, February 20, 2004, I stopped to see a client who also is an insurance agent to talk about getting insurance for the new firm. Before I entered his office, Dwight called and told me that he'd just received a call from Buster, who had received a call from Konrad, asking about me renting his office. There it was ... the cat was out of the bag! I'd been discovered!

When I reached the office, I didn't even get to sit down before being called into a meeting with all of my partners. During that meeting, I was told that I was done at the firm. I asked Konrad what he wanted me to do about my files since, from his perspective, all the clients were "firm" clients. We agreed that I would call everyone with an active file and ask if they wanted to stay or leave with me. I left the meeting, walked to my assistant to let her know that I was fired (she was fired right after me), and went to my office to begin calling my clients. All of my clients authorized me to take their files with me. Once I finished making the calls, I set out to pack up my office and eight years' worth of my professional life. My husband dropped the boys off at my parents' house, went to the local U-Haul office, and picked up some boxes for me to use.

Surprisingly, my attitude kept improving as the day wore on.

It felt like someone had lifted a weight off my shoulders and I began to smile. By day's end, I was beaming with joy. That afternoon, I left my old firm with a huge smile on my face, two months' worth of work, and immense determination to make it on my own.

On Sunday, February 22nd, we celebrated Tony's second birthday. The next morning, Ruffi Law Offices, S.C. opened its doors with no furniture, an old laptop computer, a borrowed laser printer, and a cell phone. But we were happy and I was free!

Dwight and I originally envisioned me walking out of my old firm and into my new firm with everything ready to go. Well, it didn't quite work out that way. As it turned out, our carpeting was installed the week I was fired, but we had no furniture, computers, or phones. Our furniture arrived that first day, phones were installed the following week, and the computers came a week later. We have never looked back!

Shortly after going out on my own, I called one of my old partners who had moved to Florida two years earlier. She wasn't a bit surprised when I told her the news.

Unbeknownst to me, those same partners had done the same thing to her when she worked part-time with small children. Knowing I wouldn't put up with it, she'd wondered how long it would take me to leave once I had children.

Well, it took me less than two years after becoming a mom to be done putting my job ahead of my family. My family became my main priority, practicing law my profession. Our marriage improved dramatically, and we welcomed our third son, Nic, shortly after the firm celebrated its first anniversary. Two and a half years later, Joey became son number four.

While the number of female attorneys is on the rise, the practice of law is still a male-dominated profession. I want you to know, you don't need to give up your personal life to be a quality lawyer.   In fact, in 2017 and 2018, the American Bar Association held summits to do more research on women lawyers and why they leave the practice of law.
(See Report on the National Summit Held at Harvard Law School (Nov. 2017), ABA Presidential Initiative on Achieving Long-Term Careers for Women in the Law.)

You also don't need to quit practicing law to have a happy home. You **can** be a wife, a mother, a lover, and a lawyer.
Life needn't be a struggle between two seemingly incompatible worlds.

"The secret to happiness is freedom ... And the secret to freedom is courage."
Thucydides

This book will help you gain the courage to seek your freedom, design your career to fit your life and be happy in both worlds. All you need to do is: decide, commit & succeed.

Sarah

Networking Is a Lifestyle

"Networking is the No.1 unwritten rule of success in business."
Sallie Krawcheck

Are you a busy woman, mother, and executive all wrapped in one? Do you need to network as part of your job? Do you have to juggle networking events with family time? Maddening, isn't it? Well, I have good news, friend.
Those days are gone!

Consultants tell you that you need three client development contacts per week to maintain your business and five per week to grow it. They remind you it's even more critical that you manage your connections when you're busy.

I totally agree with them. The question rests in how you define "client development contacts." My opinion and perspective on that definition have changed dramatically over the years. When I first learned this "formula," I tended to client development during the day, considering lunch meetings, business associations, and volunteering as client development time. I made sure that my calendar included at least three blocks of client development time each week. I still do those things.

However, I realized that **networking is about planting and nurturing relationships**, not collecting contacts, and I do substantially more client development than what I see on my calendar. I changed my mindset — and that changed my life.

Dr. Ivan Misner, the founder of BNI, held a similar view of networking. He maintained that "networking is more about farming than it is about hunting. It's about cultivating relationships."

11

If networking is about cultivating and building relationships —and it is— meeting with clients, referral sources, and prospective clients all happen as part of everyday life. The secret rests in recognizing this simple principle. Then, you can just DO it! (Thank you, NIKE.)

My husband and I strive to work with people who work with us. When we need something, we first ask ourselves, "Could any of our clients help here?" The photographer, florist, and planner for our wedding were all clients of mine. When my husband built our house, we looked to clients first for subcontractors in the trades; plumbing, electrical, drywalling, excavation, and contracted labor. It's a given at our house. Everywhere we go, we are working with clients or potential clients.

The primary goal is to be first in peoples' minds when they (or someone they know) need what you have to offer.

The best way to be at the forefront of people's thinking is to establish solid, trusting relationships with them. That's the result of unselfishness, even selflessness. Give to the community and the community will give back. That's just how it works. By applying the Law of Attraction, the more you give, the more you receive.

Simply put, the Law of Attraction maintains that all of our thoughts eventually become our reality. Essentially, we all can attract into our lives the things we focus on and desire.
It follows the maxim: where focus goes, energy flows. If you focus on negativity, you will find and receive more negativity. If you focus on positivity and set goals, you will find a way to achieve them by taking action. Like Lao Tzu said, "a journey of a thousand miles begins with a single step."

Take the first step (if you haven't already done so) and work to cultivate your relationships every day. Once it becomes a habit, you will notice your client base growing as well.

People buy from people they trust and respect. Be that person, and make sure that they know what you have to offer.

Every person you meet is a prospective client or referral source, either now or in the future. If a person isn't appropriate for a client now, they may be a referral source for you – provided they know what you do or have to offer, or they may need your services in the future. It's best to make sure they know all the ways you help your clients.

Some years ago, I represented a client in a collection action. We zealously represented him and obtained a good result. But I left work on the table by not showcasing the other services we offered. This client owns a construction business, working side-by-side with his son. When the day came, they chose another local attorney to draft their succession plan. Why? They didn't know I could have helped them. Now, I'm careful to educate our clients about the many ways we can help them.

You never know how your next client will find you. You may meet at the grocery store, at a park, at your children's school, at a sporting event, in an airplane, even as part of a lawsuit.

When I was a relatively new attorney, I had a client who purchased a load of hardwood. When the lumber arrived, it was not as they expected, so they rejected it. The seller refused to take the lumber back. My client refused to pay for the lumber, and the seller sued. During the lawsuit, I took the depositions of the two owners of the other company. Determined to prove my case, I didn't believe anything the guys said. Relentless and zealous, we ended up settling the case shortly before trial.

About ten years later, one of those two owners called my office with a problem but didn't identify himself during the first two calls. During the third call, he finally identified himself and asked if I remembered him, which I did. He went on to tell me, "You almost made me cry during my deposition! I knew then that if I ever needed a lawyer, it would be you."

Finding me was no small feat; I had gotten married, changed my last name, and opened my own firm since the lawsuit ended. Though I was ruthless, I still landed a client. I've handled some cases for this gentleman. It's nice to know anyone can become a client, even when you meet on opposing sides of a lawsuit.

Be Present.

We live in a community of about 100,000 people in Central Wisconsin. We patronize local businesses, regularly talk to the owners, and inquire about their business. Our grocery store owners bought their store a couple of years ago after having worked there for about 20 years. Their regular employees all know I'm an attorney and the name of our firm.

Shortly before Christmas, one of the cashiers called our office because she needed some work done quickly. Our team promptly, professionally, and compassionately helped her. A couple of months later, I went through that particular cashier's line, and she complimented me on how well our team did. I smiled and mentioned that we believe in treating our clients the way we want people to treat us. She replied, "They did exactly that!" Part of the beauty in that exchange was my decision to be fully present in the interaction with the cashier.

Rather than merely going through the motions, make a conscious decision to always be present in conversations, no matter how brief they may be. As Jim Elliot said, "Wherever you are, be all there."

To be all there, practice mindfulness. This is the basic human ability to be fully present, aware of where we are and what we are doing. When we are mindful, we do not overreact or become overwhelmed by what is happening around us.

If you have trouble calming the voices in your head so you can be present, you may want to try meditation. When I first tried it, I couldn't quiet my brain long enough to feel relaxed. However, as with everything, the more I meditated, the more comfortable and more enjoyable it became. Eventually, meditation became part of my daily routine. Sometimes, I even meditate more than once a day. It empowers me by reminding me to simply be present and breathe.

Take pride in and enjoy your work.

My husband takes pride in decorating our office inside and out to make it stand out as an inviting place to visit. In the spring, one can see colorful pinwheels spinning in the trees in front of our office. We have fun, and the exterior of our firm sets the stage. At Christmas time, strings of lights and garland grace the pillars on our porch and the stair railings. You could almost compare it to a beautifully wrapped gift.

One freezing January weekend, my husband and a couple of our sons designed and made a silhouette of Mary Poppins from a 4' x 8' sheet of plywood. That spring, Mary Poppins appeared on the East wall of our office, and she's been flying about the neighborhood ever since, letting the community know it's not business as usual for us. Mary Poppins exemplifies the welcoming and comforting atmosphere that we provide all who enter our office while bringing significant publicity and attention to our firm, including as a Pokémon Go stop. It no longer surprises us when people comment around town that they love Mary Poppins or when people know exactly where we're located when we respond to their inquiry, "We have the Mary Poppins building."

We even received a handwritten note one December from someone who lives about four blocks from the office. Our decorations brought her joy daily, and she wanted to let us know it. Her note read:

> Hello, I just want to thank you for helping my days be bright. Mary Poppins on your office makes me smile every time I drive by and your Holiday Lights are very nice to see on my way home from work. I live up the hill.
> God bless you.
> Sue

Everyone sees your building's exterior and wonders what is inside. Is it welcoming? Does it feel like a place you want to enter? Or do you have dragons and swords on the outside of your building where people think if they step inside your business, they will get devoured — and so will their money. Let them know what to expect when they cross the threshold to your reception area.

Make your clients feel comfortable and safe.

People already fighting a war don't want to start a second by going into an office that feels adversarial, especially if that office is supposed to represent them. Put yourself in your client's shoes every time they walk through your office door. It's part of building attorney-client trust.

Don't get caught up in your own world. Come around to your client's side of the table. Be present and be ready to help. Greet them with the attitude of "How may I serve?"

Dr. Wayne Dyer lived and taught this principle. When we think of others first, we experience internal joy and happiness. Think of how you feel when you hold the door open for a stranger or perform a simple random act of kindness. Personally, those simple acts bring a smile to my face and warm my heart. Follow this philosophy when handling your clients. Your clients will feel and appreciate the compassion.

When you shift your networking mindset from "it's an event" to "it's a way of life," life changes. Networking becomes your all day, everyday lifestyle, not just part of your job.

How? You ask. It's simple.

Apply the Golden Rule to life – all of it. Because "networking that matters is helping people achieve their goals." -Seth Godin

After all, your clients retain you with a goal in mind: for you to handle their current issue. Be confident, kind, and compassionate in the process, and you will be rewarded by more than their payments.

Live by the Golden Rule

"Do unto others as you would have them do unto you."
Matthew 7:12

Treat others the way you want them to treat you. We're taught that as kids. But as adults, we sometimes forget to apply it.

When it comes to networking as a way of life, following the Golden Rule vaporizes the pressure to network. People begin to think of you as a networking genius. Ironic, in a way, isn't it? Here's how it works.

> **Listen.**
>
> **Be Honest.**
>
> **Be Responsive.**
>
> **Show Appreciation.**
>
> **Be Yourself.**

Listen.

First and foremost, listen. We have two ears and one mouth for a reason; we're designed to listen twice as much as we talk. Everyone loves to talk about themselves;
slow down long enough to listen to them.

Dale Carnegie taught that the best way to sell your products or services is to understand the customer. The best way to understand the customer is to ask questions and learn all you can about them. Take a genuine interest. Find similarities and differences. Actively listen during a conversation.
People know when you listen to them. Don't spend your time thinking about your next comment or question, or how to interject about yourself. Listen.

People tell me that I am easy to talk to. Maybe that's because I let them talk without interruption. I allow others to steer the course of the conversation, offering positive input or an optimistic perspective. I try to convey a non-judgmental view of others. So can you. When you listen to those around you and offer helpful guidance or suggestions, people find you friendly. It starts with a smile or a kind gesture and a willingness to give another human being a little of your time.

It can be as simple as opening a door or giving someone directions to the nearest restroom. Yes, the restroom! I once received advice that when you go to a networking event, you always want to be perceived as helpful. So, whenever anyone asks you something, even if it's directions to the restroom, smile as you answer. When you do, they'll perceive you as helpful and kind, even if your answer happens to be "I don't know, but ...". If you offer guidance of any sort, you come across as helpful, friendly, trustworthy, and compassionate.

I always like to have "how may I serve?" idling in the back of my mind, and I continually search for opportunities and ways to answer that question. People enjoy working with people they like, and being a good listener is a great start. It's pretty easy when you take a genuine interest in people.

Less than a year after losing her husband, an elderly client retained me to remove her husband's name from the title to their home. Since she was unable to leave her home, I made a house call. Well, I actually made a couple house calls for this client. The first time I stopped, I listened to her tell stories for over three hours, though I could have gathered the information I needed in about thirty minutes. She commented that I am so easy to talk to, and under different circumstances, she could see us being really good friends. Mind you, I contributed perhaps five minutes of conversation, compared to nearly three and a half hours of listening to her stories. Most would have cut this woman off after less than an hour and been on their way. But I chose to listen, and about two hours into our first visit, she shared that it was her husband's birthday, the first one he wasn't there to celebrate with her.

During our second visit, she told me that day was the fourth anniversary of the day she nearly died. Toward the end of the second meeting, she commented that some of her friends asked how this lawyer that only one of her friends knew was taking care of her. Her response? "I couldn't ask for a better lawyer, and I'm very satisfied." She let me know that the friend who referred her to me didn't lead her wrong. In fact, the woman who recommended me did so because I also listened to her and her mother when no one else did. Moments like this confirm that I am living on purpose. They also confirm that being compassionate is a huge part of being a top notch lawyer.

Bottom line: everyone wants to be heard. Being kind and compassionate when listening to someone's concerns and sorrows can go a long way. The simple act of listening can make a world of difference for everyone you encounter, especially when your non-verbals are consistent with your words. Be prepared to hand a client a tissue or give them a hug. It is called being human.

Be Honest.

How many lawyer jokes have you heard? I let people know that rather than take offense, I grade the jokes, and I proudly share my favorite lawyer joke:

Q: What's the difference between a female attorney and a pit bull?
A: Lipstick.

Mind you, this has been my favorite joke for a long time. Shortly after I started practicing law, a client faxed a couple pages of lawyer jokes to my former boss/partner over lunch one day. I read all of the jokes before putting the fax on my boss' desk. This one stuck in my mind and has proven quite helpful over the years.

Lawyers have a reputation for being less than honest. Think about the exchange in the Jim Carey movie, Liar Liar:

> Teacher: "We're going to share what our parents do for work."
> Son: "My mom's a teacher."
> Teacher: "And your dad?"
> Son: "A liar."
> Teacher: "You mean a lawyer?"
> Son shrugs.

No one likes a liar or anyone they perceive as shady, untrustworthy, or dishonest. The adage that honesty is the best policy still holds true today, especially with the prevalence of social media.

While it may not be easy to deliver bad news or something a person doesn't want to hear, being open and honest from the outset generally saves everyone —you included— a lot of grief or a potential malpractice claim.

As lawyers, clients come to us because they have an issue and don't know how to handle or resolve it. The best way to build credibility is to avoid sugar coating your interpretation of the situation, potential outcomes, and your outlook. Learn how to give bad news as well as you deliver good news and don't be shy with the truth. It takes courage to tell a client that their outlook is not as promising as they would like, but it is much better to be open and honest at the outset. You never want to oversell a position to your client and then have to backtrack if the inevitable occurs. If you do, you lose credibility.

An elderly couple sold their cottage on a lake in Northern Wisconsin to a father and son. The 1950s cottage had a dirt crawlspace. The couple disclosed that they had hired a contractor to replace the roof and remodel the bathroom, including replacing the floor joists over the well pit. The father (buyer), a self-proclaimed construction expert, was confident a home inspector wouldn't find anything that he didn't notice. No realtor was involved. An attorney in my office handled the transaction on behalf of the elderly couple. They completed the Real Estate Condition Report, and being unaware of any defects, did not disclose any. The buyers did not have any inspections done. Soon after closing the purchase, the buyers hired an excavator to lift the cottage to build a new crawlspace, including a concrete floor, under the cottage. After removing some siding and lifting a section of the cottage, the buyers discovered that some of the floor joists were rotten. According to the excavator, the cottage was not salvageable.

The buyers hired a lawyer who sent a letter to the sellers demanding that they return about 65% of the purchase price to the buyers, claiming the sellers knew about the defects when they completed the Real Estate Condition Report. During the case, we learned that the buyer wanted to borrow money to remodel the cottage. The buyers' bank had an appraisal done to determine how much the property, including the cottage, was worth. According to the appraisal, the value of the cottage and property exceeded the purchase price and the cottage constituted only 10% of the total value. The real estate and dock constituted the remaining 90% of the value. The buyers filed a lawsuit (which never should have been filed) wanting a large sum of money to settle and refused to lower their demands.

We believed that the buyers' attorney had painted an unrealistic picture to his clients, including what their case was worth, making it extremely difficult to resolve the case. The buyers dug in their heels and were completely unrealistic.

The stress of the lawsuit aged our elderly clients about ten years in less than a year, including causing serious health issues for both.

Shortly before trial, our clients were willing to pay the buyers' original demand simply to end the stress for fear that one or both of the sellers would not survive the trial. This resulted in a settlement amount that was higher than we advised our clients to pay, but our clients decided to buy their peace in the hope of improving their health.

If the buyers' attorneys had been honest in the beginning, the buyers could have put some money in their pockets rather than paying it all to their lawyers. Not only did the lawyers' actions diminish their credibility with our office, it probably resulted in unhappy clients too.

In contrast, our firm maintained an open and honest line of communication with our clients throughout the entire process, including the cost of potential attorney fees to defend themselves.

We laid out a strategy. The most challenging aspect of the case occurred the month before trial. We explained to our clients the risks and expense of going through a jury trial. We put a plan together to gain leverage to force what we perceived to be a reasonable settlement figure. We devised a game plan that would result in our clients spending less, including attorney fees, than the amount they offered at mediation. While they understood, our clients chose to reject our proposal and pay the buyers more than half of their extortion demand. Despite writing a large check, our clients were happy with our representation because we did our best and were completely honest the entire time. Be honest. Always.

Be Responsive.

Responsiveness accompanies good listening. When you truly listen to your clients, you will understand and appreciate their position. Once you figure that out, you will be better able to add value. Listening, regardless of your profession, goes along with all aspects of the business.

In March of 2016, I was on a short flight from Central Wisconsin Airport to Chicago O'Hare. Since the plane was not very full, the flight attendant announced that three people between rows 7 and 10 needed to move toward the back of the airplane before we could take off. I was the third person to move. I gave up my seat in row 9 and ended up sitting next to a businessman in an exit row. I started our conversation by telling him that I had never been asked to move seats because the plane was too empty! I told him about the scariest flight I had ever taken, a flight out of New York on a hot August afternoon. After leaving the gate, the captain turned off the engines and announced that the plane was overloaded. After forty-five minutes without any doors or cargo hatches opening or closing, and with no air circulating in the cabin, the captain came back over the loudspeaker and miraculously announced that we were ready to go. Taxiing down the runway, we weren't sure if the plane would take off! When the wheels finally hit the tarmac in New Hampshire, I think everyone breathed a huge sigh of relief.

"Why were you going to New Hampshire?" he asked. I answered that my husband decided our firm needed a classic car, so he bought one on eBay at 2:00 a.m. on a Wednesday and two days later we flew out to pick it up and drive it home.

This man then proceeded to tell me that he also collects classic cars. For forty-five minutes he talked about himself and his businesses. When he got around to asking me what I do, I replied that I am a lawyer and help businesses. He opened up still more. He told me about how he and his lawyer were planning to create a couple of limited liability companies to protect him and his wife. Before we landed, I shared my suggestion of how he could best protect himself by structuring multiple limited liability companies and how they would impact each other. As we taxied to the gate in Chicago, he asked if I had a business card. I gave him one, and he promised to call me when I returned to Wausau.

He called about a month later, and rather than making him travel to my office, I drove about an hour to his. Following my presentation and proposal, I walked away with a $10,000 project and a check in my hand. This new client was the result of me **listening** and being **responsive** to his situation without any expectation of generating a new client.

Show Appreciation.

"Trade your expectation for appreciation, and the world changes instantly," according to Tony Robbins. This works! When your customers feel genuinely appreciated, they will go the extra mile for your product or service.

Remember, people like working with people that they like and trust. Focus on education, not selling, and your practice will improve naturally. When's the last time that you picked up the phone or sent a text message to someone and asked how their day was going, called to wish them a great day and let them know that you were thinking about them — without any expectations?

I can't count the number of times I've called someone without any idea of what is happening in their life and the conversation reveals some way that I can help, providing value at that moment.

Knowing that one of my largest clients was feeling underappreciated by her employer, I sent her a bouquet of bright, cheerful flowers. I received a delightful e-mail expressing her amazement and gratitude because we took the time to make her day.

People won't remember specific parts of conversations, but they will remember when you were the only one there for them or when you went the extra mile for them. After all, "people may not remember exactly what you said, but they will never forget how you made them feel." Maya Angelou

Be Yourself.

Masks and facades only last a limited time. If you create an image of who you are, eventually, you will experience a conflict between your true self and your image. So, always remain true to yourself and be consistent. You are the face of your business and people will recognize you for your value. In social media, maintain one personality instead of a private and a professional personality.

Facebook does not allow its users to have a personal profile and a professional profile because "[t]he days of having a different image for your work friends or co-workers and for the other people you know are probably coming to an end pretty quickly."[2]

Never compromise your standards, integrity, or ethics. Always follow your moral compass. People like dealing with a person that, like a post in the ground who never wavers or sways to get an outcome to suit them personally.

People who know me don't have to wonder what is on my mind – because it is usually coming out of my mouth!

Don't get me wrong; I don't blurt out hurtful comments. But I do believe in being open and honest about what I am thinking whether

I am talking to clients, opposing counsel, a friend, or new acquaintance.

By being open and honest, you brand yourself as a person of integrity and authenticity. Clients appreciate not having to guess what you are thinking or if you're straightforward with them.

Clients hire lawyers to help them with things that they are unable to do on their own. When a client opens up about a problem, we have a choice to sugar-coat our advice or be frank. While each client's situation is different, they all have similar components. Every situation provides an opportunity to interpret the client's case and give feedback about it, as well as possible solutions.

A number of my clients have encountered closely held business disputes. It is interesting how similar the fact patterns and emotional patterns are when shareholders are fighting. In those instances, clients come into my office frustrated, hurt, angry, and dejected. During those times, I assume the role of counselor rather than lawyer or attorney. Why? Because in those moments, my clients need someone to listen, understand, and empathize with them.

Over the years, I have had several clients go through the pain and stress of a family business crumbling around them. My first client to go through this experience owned the family business with two of his brothers. They were the third generation in the family business. Each of the brothers owned one-third of the outstanding stock in the business. One of the brothers was an alcoholic and caused major problems when he showed up at work. The other two brothers decided that he needed to leave the business. For several months, we worked on structuring a deal for the business to purchase the alcoholic brother's shares of stock. During those months, my client occupied a chair in my office for at least one hour every day. Most of the time, he simply talked about what was happening and his frustration. Essentially, I was his therapist. When we finally closed the deal, he wasn't sure how he would spend his days without his "therapy session."

That scenario has repeated itself in my office over the years. Whether I have time or not, when a client walks into my office in distress during a lengthy matter and I am available, I generally meet with them. It doesn't matter if I give them any legal advice or just a friendly listening ear, they typically leave my office in a much better mood.

The pressure to network vaporizes when you consistently apply the Golden Rule to your business. Continually working with people at various levels —with the things we've discussed here— some of them will come to regard you as a networking genius!

You're not; it's just that networking comes naturally when you make it a way of life. I encourage you to do what I did. Change your mind — and change your life.

You can have it all. Your practice. Your life. Your way!
You can be happy in both worlds.

Design Your Practice

"Nobody sets the rules but you. You can design your own life."
Carrie-Anne Moss

Owning your practice brings privileges and responsibilities that are only a dream for many.

You get to:
   design your practice.
   select your area of specialty.
   target your clientele
   choose the industry segment
on which you'll focus.

You also get to choose how your practice looks and feels.

Basically, you get to design everything about your office:

     Décor
     Dress code
     Demeanor
     Differentiator

> **Yours is the privilege and the responsibility of designing your office**
>
> **Décor**
>
> **Dress code**
>
> **Demeanor**
>
> **Differentiator**
>
> **to reflect your personality and set your clients at ease.**

Décor

One of the easiest ways to balance your work and personal life is by melding the two together. If you work full-time, you spend as much time in your office as you do at home – some weeks more.

Your office should reflect your personality. It should also appeal to the type of client you want to attract. How does your office invite people to come through your doors and immediately feel comfortable? Go ahead, take a moment to answer this question.

If you're not satisfied with your answer, ask yourself "How should it?" "How do I want people to feel when they walk through my door?"

Let's talk about the benefits of carefully designing your practice. As you decide, make sure that it's comfortable, appropriate, and inviting to your intended clientele— and also to you, since it's your home away from home.

A while back, a new client commented upon walking through our front door, "I feel like I'm walking into a friend's home."

"Perfect," I thought, "that's by design."

Our office, an old house, was built as a single-family home, converted into a duplex, and then turned into an office. We put a lot of thought into our decorating when we updated the office before we moved in. We chose a warm and inviting color scheme. We refinished the hardwood floors to showcase the original maple floors. Some of it is birds-eye maple!

The fireplaces on each floor work. We've chosen to feature original paintings done by family and friends, along with some family pictures. The magazines reflect our personality and interests. Many of the magazines meet masculine interests, putting our male clients at ease despite the more feminine feel of the office. We have a variety of toys to entertain clients' kids. When my sons were babies, a Pack 'n Play occupied a corner in my office because I usually had a kid napping in it!

How you furnish and decorate your office reflects your personality while appealing to your clients and intended clients. In our case, "this feels like a friend's home" was a high compliment. It demonstrated we'd designed our offices well. After all, our goal is for clients to feel comfortable as soon as they walk through our doors.

As another example, if you represent wives in high asset divorces, you may want to offer coffee or tea in beautiful china cups in an elegant setting. If you represent people who were injured in accidents, you may want to make sure that you have comfortable furniture, softer lighting, and a warm environment. In short, put yourself in your clients' shoes and decorate accordingly.

Your Dress Code (Attire)

Having determined your desired environment, share your vision with your staff and discuss how office attire can reflect an atmosphere consistent with your practice design.

Including your staff in the discussion will result in more immediate buy-in, and may prove beneficial in that they'll help write the guidelines for what type of clothing is appropriate and expected. Keep the dress code brief and general enough that your staff enjoys flexibility while knowing they're in-bounds when they arrive at work.

We've chosen a relaxed, professional atmosphere. Business casual suits us well. (Did you like that little word-play?) When my team or one of my clients sees me in a suit, they instantly know, "Sarah has to go to Court or give a presentation today." Our staff can wear jeans on Friday if they choose, so long as they don't look dirty or worn out. I draw the line at holes or rips in jeans, tennis shoes and flip-flops.

Many offices today have incorporated business casual. When I was leaving a meeting at an international accounting firm one day, I noticed a woman walking into work wearing flip-flops. While escorting a gentleman and me to the elevator, the managing partner of the firm and I had a discussion about what was appropriate attire in their firm, which happens to be the largest accounting firm in our area. He commented that he loves being able to wear blue jeans to work every day, which he was. He also said that he does not like flip-flops because they make too much noise. However, the firm's HR department approved flip-flops once they had a little "bling."

I responded, "I didn't realize that 'Business Casual' meant 'Casual.'" He agreed but had been overruled. I, on the other hand, have the power to draw my line of no flip-flops and enforce it. I believe that my clients would have the same reaction to flip-flops that I had, which was not a positive one.

What are your requirements or parameters? Have you ever stopped to consider them?

Relaxed professional works for us. It's by design. What does —or will— your office attire look like? Will it allow you and your staff to feel at ease while being inviting to your intended clientele? That's design applied to attire.

Your Demeanor (Mood)

In addition to the furnishings in your office, determine the type of environment you want to portray and intentionally weave it into the norm of every day.

One of my assistants let us know that her dad is a farmer and doesn't like attorneys at all. However, he would come into our office and do business with us because we are "for everyday people." People often comment that we are easy to talk to, understanding, and our office reflects this comfortable atmosphere.

That's by design. We decided at the outset that Ruffi Law would be a warm and caring place. I was done with "Impress, stress, and press" and wanted to serve my clients with skill, warmth, and empathy. I've never regretted that choice.

I remember one client who sold products to another local law firm, as well as mine. Though the other firm was big and prestigious, she chose us to represent her when she decided to sell her business. We went to lunch after the deal closed to celebrate and to review things.

I asked her why she chose to use us and how she would rate her experience working with us.

In answering, she painted me a picture contrasting our firm to Firm X. She shared that when she called on Firm X, she felt the need to be sure that her hair and makeup were perfect and her clothes looked professional. She checked her posture as she walked in so she was prim and proper; their overall appearance and attitude felt uptight and stuffy. At our firm, she could be herself. She didn't have to put on a snooty air or worry about her appearance. She knew that when she walked through the door, she'd be greeted with a warm smile and a friendly "Hello." No pretense or fake appearance, just compassion, family, and quality advice where she could be herself.

After we sold her business, she left the following 5-star Google review:

"Sarah was referred to me by a colleague who said she'd be an excellent choice as my business attorney, and she was! Sarah presented as intelligent, fair, honest, and direct. She guided me through the process of selling my business, and when I had questions, she was there to explain in terms I could understand. The sale went very smoothly and efficiently. Thank you, Sarah!"

Intentionally choose your office demeanor and work to maintain it.

One more thing. No matter the market segment you're serving, show your clients compassion. If you don't show them the love, they'll farm their work out to a firm that does.

Your Differentiator

Is there something about your practice that makes you different from all the rest?

It doesn't have to be grandiose, just something that differentiates you from all the other law firms that come up when you Google "attorney." That differentiator (or X factor) makes you easy to remember, and it can be fun!

A unique part of our office is our upstairs bathroom. It was probably last updated in the mid-1950s or 1960s, so the walls are a shiny mauve/pink color, and the tiles are "this lovely pink" (NOT!). Rather than gut and remodel that bathroom, Dwight decided to create our own unique wallpaper by plastering positive, motivational quotes on the walls. We have clients who specifically ask to use that bathroom before they leave because they love reading the quotes! When we get sick of the design (or have read the quotes too many times), we rip off the quotes and start again.

At one point, we had a sheet of paper with words like understanding, strength, compassion, love, and honesty on strips that could be torn off. The top said: "Take what you need." One day, one of my clients came out of the bathroom and showed me the word that she tore off the sheet. That one word summarized our conversation that day: Strength. She took it home with her.

Your Differentiator doesn't just have to be about your office set up. In addition to clients feeling comfortable in your office, they can become a part of your personal life too.

We have built our business on the premise that "we work with people who work with us." As a business lawyer, I have come in contact with many people from all walks of life, and a variety of industries. Since our clients trust us with their legal matters, including financial and confidential information, they are the first place we look when we need something done. We patronize our clients' businesses for everything from where we go to eat, to whom we use for contracted services (plumbing, heating, electrical, construction projects), who handles our insurance, where we bank, who designs our marketing material, delivers our flowers and bakes our birthday cakes. We could do business differently and bypass clients for cheaper goods or services, but in return, they could do the same.

Remember what you give – you receive. Period.
It's business. It's personal. It's Life.
You will come to regard yourself as a networking genius! You're not. It's just that when it's a way of life, networking is easier than you imagined. I encourage you to do what I did.
Change your mind and change your life

You can have it all. Your practice. Your life. Your way!
You can be happy ... (Go ahead. Finish it.) Exactly.

Build a Strong Team

"Find the smartest people you can and surround yourself with them."
Marissa Meyer, CEO Yahoo

Let's talk about your team.

Not the one you're on and maybe wish you weren't.

Not the great team you used to be on.

Let's talk about the team you're going to build.

The one you'll lead.

> **Strong teams have four things in common:**
>
> **Pattern**
>
> **Professional**
>
> **Particular**
>
> **Perspective.**

Your team.
It needs to be strong.
It needs to excel.

How you build it makes all the difference in the world.

We'll discuss four Ps in this chapter:

Pattern
Professional
Particular
Perspective.

They'll work together to make perfect sense as you read. Ready? Let's go.

Pattern

Teams are constructed to accomplish specific tasks. Win ball games. Design new products. Execute corporate turnarounds or comebacks. Plan events – even clean up after them.

Before you pick your team, you need to create its pattern with answers to questions like:

What will your team DO?

What are your core values?

What is your culture?

With that in mind, it's time to find people that fit that team, play that position. Look for the best you can find, while being authentic. It's easy to think that if we use a successful person's formula to find and hire employees, we'll somehow tap into magic, and everything will be great with our new hires. My advice: draw on best practices but be true to yourself. When hiring, hire the person who fits your firm, not just the person who can fill the position.

For example, when we interview, we use humor. We're relaxed. We are not politically correct; we go with the flow. Why? Because that's how we are. It's who we are. That's how we'll be their 2nd week, and 2nd year on the job. We look for flexibility. We want to know: Are they smart? Can they go with the flow? Most importantly, will they fit in our firm? Those are the things we notice and the questions we want to be answered in a particular way.

Professional

Identify your top three character traits as it relates to professionalism and don't compromise in your search for them in a new team member. You can train to add skills, but you can't renovate character – or add it later. Character walks through the door with each new hire. Make sure it matches your criteria and culture. Bear in mind, as people get more comfortable, their true character will begin to show. Make sure their genuineness fits your firm.

Our top three are
   trust,
   compassion,
   and integrity.

First and foremost is trust. Do you have high standards? Can we trust you? Will our clients be able to trust you and feel comfortable sharing their issues with you?

Trust is the most expensive thing in the world. It can take years to develop and seconds to destroy. Don't let a lack of trust destroy you or your firm.

An attorney-client relationship thrives when people trust their attorney and her team. It's non-negotiable for us; it should be for you too. If an employee lacks high standards, it will always show, but not necessarily during the interview process. In those situations, we follow the approach of firing fast. We once had an employee who made it through our hiring process with flying colors from everyone. However, on her first day of work, her attitude and demeanor changed. She asked an uncomfortable number of questions about clients and what work we did for them, including past work, simply because she saw their names in the system. My paralegal did not feel comfortable leaving this employee at a computer by herself. Needless to say, she lasted less than two days in our firm before we let her go because we could not trust her.

Second, compassion. Are you a caring individual? Our clients bring us problems and ask for our help. Our team needs to care. Not because they're paid to, but because it's who they are. When you listen and empathize with your clients, they know you care and feel as though the weight has been lifted off their shoulders. How often do your clients leave with the departing comment that "I feel better" or "I know that I'm in good hands" or "I will sleep better tonight"? Those feelings come from a sense of gratitude after being treated with compassion by their lawyer.

Third, are you a person of integrity? Are you open? Honest? Integrity means doing the right thing, even when no one is watching.

Before becoming President, General Dwight D. Eisenhower demonstrated integrity. Before storming the beaches of Normandy, General Eisenhower drafted a message to the public in case the Allies were defeated. Fortunately, the Allies' plans worked.

His letter read:

> "Our landings in the Cherbourg-Havre area have failed to gain a satisfactory foothold, and I have withdrawn the troops. My decision to attack at this time and place was based upon the best information available. The troops, the air, and the Navy did all that bravery and devotion to duty could do. If any blame or fault attaches to the attempt, it is mine alone."

General Eisenhower knew the risks when he sent 160,000 troops from the United States, Great Britain, France, Canada, and other nations to face the Germans on the beaches of Normandy on June 6, 1944. He was following orders, but he, alone, accepted responsibility for the outcome. A person with integrity accepts 100% responsibility for every situation, even if a scapegoat may be available. That is integrity.

Other contributing factors include the confidence to put your best foot forward. Confidence does not mean that you must know the answer. It means that you're willing to go find it. Don't intimidate your client, give him answers.

But −I learned this lesson a long time ago− if you give your answers too fast, it can result in less trust. As a young lawyer, I had a client tell me that he wasn't sure he trusted me. When I asked why, he said that I answered his questions too quickly. At that point, I consciously changed how I respond.

Since then, I take a breath before I respond to anyone's questions —not just a client's— even when I know the answer. That way, the client knows that I heard the question/issue, thought about it, formulated an informed response, then answered. If that helps build trust with confidence, so be it.

Think of your client - that's service. Are you a giver? How many people serve you? You should serve more. Live life from the perspective of "how may I serve?" Your clients will feel it and the corresponding trust that accompanies it will grow.

Particular

You need to be particular. Precise. Knowing what your team needs. In your communication, be clear and concise. Know what you communicate and how. Does your interviewee, soon to be your new team-member, know quality?

Once vetted and able to work on their own, this team-member will need to rise to the challenges that come, contributing to your team's ability to reach your objectives.

There are new challenges with the new generation, just like there were when we were new, so know its strengths. Know its general weaknesses. Work specifically within the traits as needed, calling on specific skills to reach team objectives.

When it comes to communication with your clientele, balance is necessary.

Avoid the tug of war between speed and accuracy. Are we known for being quick? Or are we known for being accurate, even though it may take longer?
The answer – Yes to both.

speed

content   vs   grammar

accuracy

The same is true of client conversations and written letters. Useful information. Well-written. Perfect? Maybe not, but excellent, for sure. Very respectable.

Perspectives

On Strategy.

Who on your team sees things from 30,000 feet?

At Ruffi Law that person is Dwight. He sees things from above. He's strategic. He is relational. In many ways, it's as though we have someone above the race, like at America's Cup, for example, observing, strategizing, telling us what to do and when, so we can gain -and maintain- our advantage.

In sports, this would be the coach in the Press Box looking at things objectively from above. You need someone on your team, able to see things from that vantage point. Often, we get so close to the situation that we can't see the forest because of the trees, as the saying goes. A well-balanced team has the person who can pull you out of the situation to regain your perspective.

Numerous times over the years, Dwight has anticipated our work flow and pushed me to hire a new team member before I felt I was ready. However, he had the perspective and insight to know when we needed the next person BEFORE the tidal wave hit. I kept my focus on making sure the work product headed out the door and simply worked more instead of thinking about adding more people to lighten my load. Thank goodness for Dwight and his 30,000 foot view.

On Team Roles.

What's your role as the firm owner?

It helps to identify it in your own thinking first, and then with your team. Clarity in defining your role is vital and must precede defining other team roles.

When I first began to build my team, I thought I could be friends with everyone on my team.

That doesn't work. I can be friendly, but being everyone's friend is not my role. Remember, you are building a professional team, not a sports team. There are similarities, but they are fundamentally different teams. Over the years, Dwight and I have found a balance that works for us. I maintain the professional boss role while Dwight is more friendly. Our team members tell Dwight way more than they tell me, which works for us.

When I onboard a new member as I build my team, I emphasize:

You have a compassionate leader, that's me,
but I'm a leader first, compassionate second.

You have a cheerleader. I will pull for you, but I'm not your parent.

I am a parent to my four boys and the numerous exchange students we have hosted from around the world. They'll be around; I hope that's okay with you.

Your work begins before you start, just as mine did, preparing to bring you on.

It's my responsibility to set you up to succeed. When you came into the office for your first day of onboarding, you had login information. You had business cards. You had a place to work. You were set. I expect you to approach our clients similarly. Your work begins before you start.

When we bring new associates on board, especially if they are new to the area, we require them to join five, yes five, service organizations within the first month of employment. They cannot simply join the organizations, either. They need to become active members and move into leadership roles. The purpose of the requirement is two-fold. First, show the people in the organization that when they say they will do something, they do it. Second, become part of the community, not an outsider.

One of our associates moved to Wausau from Madison with the sole intention of working for a year and then moving back to Madison. He became actively involved in several service organizations, including accepting Board positions in each of them shortly after joining. Despite his intention to return to Madison, Wausau became his home. If we did not require him to join the organizations to connect with the community, he might well have returned to Madison.

On Balancing Individual Concerns with Team Concerns

When it comes to balancing the good of the individual with the good of the team, it's not either/or with us. Both are priorities. We ask, "how can we help people?".

We invest in people (individuals) for the good of the team (collective). So should you.

Everything changes, nothing remains the same. I learned a crucial lesson years ago; everyone is replaceable. Everyone, including me. One of my clients (who happened to have an office across the hall from me) shared this tip when I was having problems with my first

47

employee. I wasn't sure that I believed him until the employee quit before I could fire her. Since then, we have reminded ourselves of this lesson numerous times and will likely do so well into the future.

When you are new in business, you tend to think that you cannot survive without a certain person. Yes, you can. People come - people go - live with it, with dignity. It's business.

This is always a hard lesson to learn and remember. Every once in awhile, we also get the reminder when a team member leaves.

Individuals on your team may see certain other team members as irreplaceable. However, they adjust when a new person joins the team or a team member leaves. It is all about perspective. In fact, when a poor performing team member leaves, the atmosphere of the office tends to improve quickly after the initial shock dissipates.

It's one more reason to stay humble.

Conclusion

As you build your team, woman warrior, you must remember, you have a business, and it must move forward to remain viable. Stick to your guns. If things go wrong, you are the one that falls.

Preserve your professional honor.

Pattern

Professional

Particular

Perspective.

They work together. Make sense?

_____

For more information along the lines of teamwork, read the following people:

Jim Collins,
Tony Robbins,
Patrick Lencioni,
John Maxwell,
Jack Canfield,
Dr. Wayne Dyer.

Watch Patrick Lencioni on Teamwork:
https://youtu.be/iJTtlKV-bhQ (00:02:30)

Take Control of Your Schedule

"Control your own destiny or someone else will."
Jack Welch, Former CEO General Electric

I love being in control, don't you?
Then why is it so hard to control time?

We see it characterized as a baby and an old man every New Year's; harmless enough, even cute in a way. But where does it go when we're not looking?!

I saw this a while back, posted on my editor's blog: You'll never have more time. You have –and always have had– all there is.

We go to seminars, read self-help books, look for planners that help us do well with time, but time is always a challenge – or at least the use of it is. In this chapter, we'll focus on principles and mechanics; some critical time-centered thoughts and best practices I've come across.

In this chapter, we'll take some time to apply them to your life and practice.

When it comes to taking control of your schedule, you'll be ahead of your competition if your plan includes:

Simple Systems that are **I**ndependent, Individualized and **M**aintained.

Projects we divide and conquer, **L**everaging lawyer time and effort **E**ffectively. It actually works!

Time, as a commodity, has a unique characteristic.

It arrives at a constant rate:
    60 minutes per hour,
    24 hours per day,
    one day at a time.
Yet, we class some as productive
and some as wasteful or lost.

> It is not enough to be
> busy. So are the ants.
> The question is:
> What are we busy about?
>
> Henry David Thoreau

Q: What makes the difference?
A: Our use of the energy we spend,
    measured in minutes, hours, or days.

For most people, complicated systems for managing time compound the problem.

Have a system that is short and simple. K.I.S.S. (Keep It Short and Simple).

Routines are valuable in that they help standardize how we do things. Hopefully, you have a morning routine that carries you from the time you wake up until you get to the office.
Do you have a system intact for opening your office the same way each morning? If not, you should. Better yet, it should be written down so anyone can follow it.

By taking control of how your professional life begins, you invite order to your day. It's just like yesterday. That stability is essential to your team and your clients.

Repeatable tasks occur on schedule every day, few days, or weeks.

A simple system provides consistency when followed and allows a temporary employee or new person in that role to continue on-task and on-time. Craft simple procedures for delegated work, such as:

- Form letters with blanks to complete. This streamlines the process and standardizes your letters. If it doesn't work or stops working, change it.
- Scheduling procedures, when followed, bring consistency while minimizing scheduling errors and malpractice claims.
- Opening and closing the office should be done the same way each day.
- Standardize how you answer the phone and greet clients.
- Create procedures for opening and closing files, which includes entering information into your conflicts system.

There's no need to reinvent the wheel. If a procedure works, keep it, being sure to keep your system simple. If your system stops working, figure out what stopped working and correct it. Your team has more important things to do with their minds today than think about mundane tasks.

Allow room for **individuality**, a measure of **independence**, because not everyone on your team works the same way. Your schedule, while standardized and straightforward, should not be rigid.

Schedule the work that demands your best for the best (most productive) part of your day. Grant your team the same flexibility within defined parameters. They'll love that they can be their own person in the quest for productivity. Block and protect those productive hours. Just don't forget to identify who's to answer the phone at what times, so expectations are clear.

For example, in our firm, we have two people who answer the telephones. For them to have uninterrupted time, they work together and decide who answers the phones and when. Depending on workloads, one may answer the phone in the morning and the other in the afternoon. Or, they may switch by the day. They have the authority to decide how they will work together. As long as the phone calls are answered within two rings, all is good.

Now that you're enjoying some consistent productivity, **maintain** your approach to time and its use. Time-use, if left unattended, deteriorates and atrophies. You can't afford to let that happen.

"Life is what happens to us while we are making other plans," said Allen Saunders (Reader's Digest, 1957). It's a familiar quip, and John Lennon quoted him in his song "Beautiful Boy" (1980). But it's not how you want things to go in your firm.

Adjust your schedule if you have good reasons. It requires consistent attention, just like your budget. Your schedule IS a budget — of hours and minutes. Like money, your time is limited. Use it wisely. Be your fiercest schedule warrior and hold your work times sacred.

When a **project** comes through the door, here's a best practice to divide and conquer:

Delegate down to the lowest common denominator, i.e., the person with authority to carry out the work at the most economical rate. In my office, when there's a notice of motion to be done, for example, I delegate it. When there's a brief to write, I may delegate some of the research and drafting. A lawyer will do the brief itself.

Once completed, I delegate down the referencing and proofreading to a paralegal or legal assistant. Project processes, while not complicated, need to be defined. Delegating down is cost-effective for your clients and time-effective for you.

You can **leverage** your time by standardizing recurring tasks.

I know attorneys who read their junk mail over the wastebasket. What I want to know is, "Why did it even reach you?" My staff knows to remove certain things from the information flowing toward me. They know how to filter my mail, calls, email, and walk-ins, leveraging my time so I'm at my best.

Some call this "pre-delegating." More important than the tag you give it, is the ability and authority you give team members to execute those time-consuming tasks efficiently. By granting my staff authority to be my gatekeepers, they allow me to better control my schedule.

For example, some of today's communication with the government is forms-driven and digital. In Wisconsin, corporations and limited liability companies must file an Annual Report with the Department of Financial Institutions. We receive a post card in the mail reminding us that the Annual Report is due. When the post card arrives, a member of my team will go online and file the Annual Report. Once we receive the e-mail confirming that it was filed, we forward the email and filed report to the client so they know it was done. I do not have to touch the post card or any part of the process. It simply gets done.

In short, standardizing this recurring task leverages our time. The same can be applied to other recurring tasks.

Lastly, your time-related devices must be **effective**. With recurring but unscheduled tasks, adopt this mindset: Delegate down to the lowest capable level, with the ability to finish the job and report its completion to your standards.

When the system doesn't work, bear in mind that tweaking the procedure probably takes less time than whining about it! Just fix it and let the team know what you did. Better yet, seek their input on how to tweak your procedures. After all, team members who do the work frequently have the best perspectives on ways to improve it.

Would a little device help you remember
the main points of this chapter?

When it comes to taking control of your schedule,
you'll have an advantage if your plan includes:

> **S**imple Systems that are
> **I**ndependent, Individualized and
> **M**aintained.
>
> **P**rojects we divide and conquer,
> **L**everaging lawyer time and effort
> **E**ffectively. It actually works!

Your schedule won't be perfect the first time. It may not be perfect the second, third, fifth, or tenth time either. Just get started and modify it as you go. Consider it a work in progress. Things change and so will your systems. Consider this a step by step process. Don't try to tackle it all at once and think you will refine it overnight. Start with baby steps. What works for me may not work for you and vice versa. After all, we all have different personalities, needs, and practices. If this paragraph just frustrated you, good. It means that I got your attention.

You may go through a lot of frustration trying to develop and implement simple processes in your practice. Have faith. Eventually, your processes will become a beautiful symphony, allowing you to sing and dance more. In turn, you will find more free time by designating your work time.

Seize the moments in your schedule
and enjoy the freedom it brings.

Delegate Effectively

*"Are we limiting our success by not mastering the art of delegation?
... it's simply a matter of preparation meeting opportunity."*
Oprah Winfrey

Lawyers burn out when they attempt to do everything by themselves, working at maximum capacity every day. 40% of lawyers suffer from anxiety, twice the rate of the general US population.[1]

I have good news for you; you don't have to be part of the 40%.

Build a team to help you out and delegate responsibilities to them. Teams produce results all around us, from restaurants to oil-changing crews, sports teams to corporations. Make your team a good one.

Definition:

To **delegate** is to entrust a task or responsibility to another person, typically one who is less senior than oneself.

Effective Delegation

Leverages Your Time and Expertise

Facilitates Your Control of Time

Provides Opportunity to Train Your Team

Everyone in the Firm Contributes

S.M.A.R.T. Delegating

Delegation is not dumping unwanted tasks on a subordinate's desk and walking away. It's more about guidance than about supervision.

---

[1] www.lawyerswithdepression.com/articles/how-stress-and-anxiety-become-depression-2/

Supervision is watching over someone to make sure they do the work and do it correctly. Guidance is training and supporting the person so, over time, the person does not require as much supervision.

Delegation is ultimately about steering.

It benefits law firms, allowing us to leverage our time and expertise.

In this chapter, we'll discuss how to realize those benefits. Here's the bottom line. Your business should be able to run without you. By delegating work to your team members, they will keep the business running even when you are off-site.

Delegation Leverages Your Time and Expertise

Delegation allows lawyers to efficiently deliver top quality work at a lower cost. Ideally, you should delegate every task that does not require your skills to the lowest level competent person to complete your work. When I meet with new clients, I let them know up front that I believe in delegating work to the person best situated to do it to my standards at the most cost-effective rate (i.e., the lowest billing rate). However, I also assure my clients that the work will be done to my standards and will be reviewed by me before it goes out the door. In so doing, my clients receive our quality product and service more economically and timely than if I were to do it all. Everyone wins.

Delegation Facilitates Your Control of Time

Having capable team members perform portions of client services work, frees you to focus on higher-level services, more significant projects, networking, and honing your business. It allows you to work on your business, not just in your business. In short, you no longer have to do everything yourself.

If you're currently uncomfortable delegating work, start small and grow. Begin with easy to explain tasks you have reduced to forms. This gives your staff experience and exposure to the practice area while you become more comfortable letting go of some work.

For instance, you have clients who call. Someone should answer those calls. You receive mail. Someone should open and process it. You need to open files, and when the matter is completed, close those files. To delegate opening files, you would assign a team member the tasks of
   a) creating the digital and paper files,
   b) adding the client and opposing party/parties to your conflict search system, and
   c) preparing a retainer/engagement agreement.

Consider how you can hand off repetitive tasks to your staff.

If yours is a litigation practice, delegate the preparation of filing letters, preparing the summons, and electronically filing documents. In a real estate practice, delegate ordering title insurance, preparing the deed and transfer return, and the letter to the Register of Deeds to record the signed deed. Think about those standard, repetitive tasks and create systems for them, which your office staff can follow.

When I decided to go out on my own, I knew that I needed an assistant. If nothing else, my assistant would answer the phone, open the mail, make copies, send out the mail, and schedule appointments. Additionally, I wanted my assistant to draft standard forms, such as Summons, Powers of Attorney, form letters, garnishment paperwork, and notices. I asked one of the assistants from my old firm who did most of my work if she wanted a new job. I didn't want to train someone new. She agreed, and after opening our new firm, I expanded her responsibilities, reducing many of my repetitive tasks. We worked as a team for nearly five years.

Free Time for Yourself

Don't get caught up in the details of simple though essential tasks.

Some tasks may take longer to explain than to complete yourself. In the long run, however, you will benefit from taking the time to teach your staff how to complete the simple tasks instead of doing them yourself. Someone on a lower pay-grade, such as your legal assistant, can perform essential but straightforward functions.

Keep your office running like a fine-tuned machine, even when you're gone. If your office requires your presence to run, you have a high-priced job. When it can run without you, you have a business.

The difference between the two rests in the systems you have in place and the training you provide to your team. After being in business for about 12 years, we tested whether I have a high-priced job, or we have a business. We took a family trip to Europe. Dwight and three of the boys spent a little under three weeks away from home. Joey and I stayed an extra week and a half to attend a wedding in Amman, Jordan. During our vacation, I had minimal contact with the office after Dwight gave the team strict instructions to NOT contact me while we were gone. They needed to figure things out on their own... and they did. When Dwight returned to the office, he had a meeting with the staff and addressed any fires that were blazing at that moment. By the time I returned, my team knew they could handle most things on their own because we gave them the authority to do so. Now, I don't hesitate to leave the office for a week-long conference or vacation.

Delegating Provides Opportunity to Train Your Team. You retain ultimate control of the work.

While I delegate work, nothing leaves the office without me reviewing and approving it. It must meet my quality standards, or it doesn't go out the door. When I draft briefs and letters, I use short, choppy sentences in an active voice to engage the reader, rather than allow the reader to observe passively. Eventually, my staff adopts the same writing style, minimizing "is, are, was, were, be, being, been" in their writing. In general, I don't allow sentences to exceed a full line. A reader shouldn't read a sentence more than once because it's too long. Over time, your staff will adopt your style as well.

Teach new associates about all aspects of your practice area.

The best way to learn something new is to do it. To properly advise a client, an attorney must understand the entire process. So, guide and mentor new associates through a file's process until they know it. One of my associates came to our firm with two years' experience in a bankruptcy firm. To my surprise, he didn't know the entire bankruptcy process! He only did specific portions of the bankruptcy filings; support staff did the repetitive parts of the work. The senior attorney didn't teach him how to do those portions of a case or explain to him how the sections all fit together. Despite having his license for two years, he didn't know what a Summons was or how to draft one! I made sure that the first litigation file he handled with us included oversight and explanations along the way of how to handle a lawsuit. Once he understood the various documents, how and why they fit in the process, he became a better litigator.

Teach your assistants the nuances of repetitive tasks to consistently reflect your style in all services.

Those little touches tend to set you apart from your competition.

**Set this book down a minute
and think about what makes you, you.**

How does your way of practicing compare to other attorneys?

What do you do differently? (your differentiator)

How do you communicate with your clients?

What is your "X-factor" when it comes to serving your clients?

Jot down your answers here:

_____

_____

_____

_____

_____

_____

_____

_____

_____

_____

_____

_____

_____

_____

Welcome back. Our staff knows that our clients hire us because they have a problem they don't know how to solve. By understanding the nuances of tasks, our team can better explain the steps of a case to our clients and can keep them well-informed as the case progresses.

For example, we use a standard form letter to explain the small claims process and what happens at the first court appearance after we file the case. Our team understands the importance of how this simple letter provides valuable information to our clients. In our process, we provide our clients with peace of mind and knowledge of the process with simple letters to explain the status of their case. These letters give the client more power and more clarity.

Explain the steps for projects you believe your team member can handle.

Before you delegate a project to a member of your team, consider that person's skill set and the types of tasks they can handle. A legal assistant may be best equipped to process mail, answer telephones, manage calendar appointments and court appearances, prepare standard form letters, organize and update client files, and prepare simple forms.

A paralegal, depending on experience, may be able to handle the legal assistant's tasks plus more advanced legal work, such as basic research, drafting documents, summarizing depositions, and processing your e-mails. Once you decide that a person can handle a particular task, take the time to explain all the steps of the project.

When I first have a person process an earnings garnishment, for example, I explain which documents to prepare, who receives which documents, how to calculate when the garnishment ends, and when we need to file the next earnings garnishment.

Delegate in writing, following a standard form.

A clear delegation form guides your team members from starting line to finish line of their assigned task. It is much easier to get from Point A to Point B when you have clear directions. To avoid breakdowns in communication, use a standard delegation form that answers the following questions:

> How did we get to this point in the case?
>
> What do I need to do?
>
> What steps will complete the task?
>
> What are the potential pitfalls, if any?
>
> When is the project/assignment due?
>
> What is the desired outcome/result?

By preparing a written delegation form, you save time. You convey information your team member might have missed in a verbal explanation. Sometimes a belts-and-suspenders approach is best, where you meet with the person to review the delegation form and answer questions before the person starts.

When I have a complex assignment, I'll sometimes meet with the person, usually an associate, to discuss the case and its background, and we'll review the delegation form together. This conversation provides the person with a fresh, in-depth understanding of the issue, and I'm right there to answer immediate questions.

Delegation provides an opportunity for seasoned lawyers to train the next generation of lawyers and support staff.

For you to focus on priority-one work, you pass other work on to your staff, delegating to those best suited to particular tasks. For example, to support staff, I assign formwork and repetitive tasks, such as drafting form letters, garnishments, small claims summons & complaints, preparing deeds and real estate transfer returns, and other standard work. When new associates start, I want them to understand those standard jobs, so they also receive such assignments. Remember the associate who joined us not knowing the basics of handling a lawsuit because support staff did all that in his previous firm? I call that a skills gap. To avoid skills gaps, I have new associates learn each aspect of the areas of law in which they practice. Furthermore, one should never delegate something that they do not know how to do.

Use a written delegation form that provides the goal to accomplish, the steps to take, potential issues/pitfalls, and a deadline. With a properly drafted delegation form, you point your team members in the right direction from the beginning. Checklists for everyday tasks boost a teammate's confidence in that they know they've left nothing out. I use checklists whenever and wherever I can. I also encourage my staff to create their own checklists.

When delegating a task to a new employee or delegating a new responsibility to an existing employee, I streamline the process by a) attaching to the delegation form sample documents they can reference or b) including the filename with its path in the form.

When I was a young associate, my boss' idea of delegating work was to verbally explain an issue to me and set me free to figure it out. Unless I took outstanding notes, important details or information would sometimes get lost in translation. Likewise, I didn't necessarily understand what steps to follow or documents to draft to complete a project.

This resulted in a lot of wasted time and needless dead ends. When I missed something, there was no way to determine whether the explanation had fallen short, or if my interpretation was to blame. Having a defined delegation system in place will close the communication gap by providing a clear picture of how you delegated the work. Was it clear? Complete? What did we miss, if anything? Delegation forms also go a long way toward avoiding the "I forgot" excuse.

After opening my own firm, I created a delegation form. It specifies what I'm delegating and to whom, along with the background of the issue. Then, we identify the steps of the project, with a deadline for each step. The form also includes areas where I spell out anticipated challenges or difficulties, along with expected outcomes. Set out standard projects in delegation forms, which can become forms.

For example, when organizing a single member limited liability company, the delegation form for my support staff includes the following steps:

☐ **Prepare**:
   ☐ Member's Statement;
   ☐ Unit Certificate;
   ☐ Record of Unit Holders;
   ☐ Subscription Agreement;
   ☐ LLC letter to client;
☐ **Enter** filing fees into the accounting system;
☐ **Prepare** statement for the client;
☐ **Call client** to schedule an appointment
   to review and sign the documents.

If the project is new to an employee, I include the file names and location to use as the basis for each document. Once the person knows the process, I simplify the form by leaving out the file names.

When creating a delegation form for a research project for an associate, the sometimes-lengthy background section of the form may even include a memorandum outlining the facts and history of the file. The steps may include the issues to research, as well as drafting notices, motions, memorandums of law, affidavits, proposed orders, and letters.

Everyone in the Firm Contributes

Every member of your team needs to contribute to the success of the firm. They may answer the telephones, manage calendars, and greet clients. Perhaps they handle the money. One may prepare standard documents and perform basic research, while another consults with the clients and engages in high-level legal analysis and drafting. No matter the skill level required, every person must engage in activities that help move work out the door and build the practice.

If a person does not contribute to the firm in a meaningful or productive manner, you have some decisions to make. Does the person need more training? Is the person a fit for the firm but in the wrong position? Is there something happening in the person's private life that is impacting their performance at work? If so, can you help resolve the problem? Does the person need help to separate that issue from affecting their job? Is this person not a fit for the firm and need to find a more suitable position for them? I learned from a business coach soon after opening Ruffi Law to hire slow and fire fast.

As cruel as it may sound, letting someone go as soon as you know they no longer fit helps both the employee and the firm. We generally follow a rather extensive hiring process. But it's not fail-proof. We once hired a young mother who seemed to have a lot to offer us. She failed to show up for work on her first day because she was hit by a bus on her way to work. On her actual first day, she started asking questions about clients and what work we did for them. She also took an unusual interest in a particular practice area outside of the work that we assigned to her. Her actions gave everyone in the office, especially my support staff, an uneasy feeling. Within a couple of days, we knew that we had made a mistake hiring her and rehabilitation didn't appear to be an option. We let her go less than two days after she started.

Everyone becomes a revenue center.

Whenever a member of your team does a task that contributes to the progress of a client's matter, capture that time and bill for it. Train your staff so they know what tasks are billable and have your employees track all they do. That way, when the time arrives to review pre-bills, you know how much to bill. Also, you have the choice to bill the time or not because your team member captured it.

Delegate SMART

You need to delegate SMART:

Specific,

Measurable,

Agreed,

Reasonable and

Timebound.

The goal is to ensure that all delegated tasks effectively cover all five elements of **SMART**, the same way a reporter covering a story answers who, what, where, when, why, and how.

Specific. Explain in detail what you want to be done, including the steps to follow. Break your delegation down as precisely and detailed as necessary for the person receiving the work. The first time I assign a task to an employee, I break it down to individual steps, including what applicable forms to use and where to find each form.

For example, when I have an assistant draft the essential documents to organize a limited liability company (LLC), I use my standard delegation form. The first few times that assistant organizes an LLC, the form identifies each required document to prepare, the name of the form, and the folder containing that form. Once the assistant understands the process, the delegation form specifies the required documents, but not document locations, as that is now understood.

Measurable. Along with being specific, track, and measure how well your staff members complete tasks. When you give specific instructions, you can gauge whether the individual is on track to meet the goal. This information enables your associate to self-assess their quality and timeliness. It will also prove essential during employee appraisals when you will need to provide detailed data about their performance.

Agreed. It's essential that your team-member agrees to do the work, understands your expectations and time constraints, and knows they have the authority connected to the task to complete it. It's up to you to know they have the knowledge, skills, training, resources, and confidence to achieve it, but their agreement to take on the project remains vital.

Reasonable. Carefully consider what you assign to your staff. Ask yourself:

> Is this part of their job description?
>
> Are my expectations reasonable?
>
> Is this attainable?"

Be careful not to overload a team member with a multitude of tasks. If you pile more on a team member than you could complete in the allotted time, your employee risks becoming discouraged, frustrated, and disgruntled. Your employee could question their competency and value to the firm. You may become a bit discouraged yourself and begin to think it would have been faster to have done the work yourself. And you'd be right – that time. However, that doesn't mean it'll be right in the future.

Timebound. Make sure you include a deadline for each step on the delegation form. When you have a major deadline, make sure that you give your staff incremental-step deadlines that ensure you'll reach your deadline with a bit of breathing room.

Don't burn yourself out. Skip the anxiety.
Delegate so you can sit down to dinner, smile across the table and announce, "My team did awesome today!"

Have a Mentor
Be a Mentor

"The question is not only who can be your mentor,
but also who can you mentor?"
Mariela Dabbah

Do you have a person you feel comfortable asking for advice?
Someone who can help you understand the technical points of
practicing law? Someone who can guide you in dealing with clients?
Someone you aspire to imitate? If not, you may be missing out.
Every lawyer needs a mentor, regardless of how long they've been
practicing.

A mentor is someone who coaches and guides another.

Mentors come in different forms and for various reasons. We can
have mentors for personal life, physical fitness, our profession, and
other endeavors. You can even have more than one mentor.

New lawyers have a learning curve that, in some ways, resembles a
sheer cliff dropping a hundred feet into the ocean. After all, once
lawyers obtain their "ticket," they have a license to give clients legal
advice and clients expect that advice to be accurate. Clients do
not generally have a ton of understanding or patience because the
attorney representing them is new. No, clients expect to receive
quality advice because they're paying for it. To navigate these
sometimes-narrow corridors, lawyers, regardless of age, benefit
from mentors. Mentors come in all shapes, sizes, and situations.

Often, young female attorneys must work hard to prove that they
earned their titles, positions, and clients' trust. As I mentioned
earlier, I had a client who didn't trust me because I answered his
questions too quickly. It didn't matter that my answers were

correct. In hindsight, this client proved to be a unique mentor. From then on, I made a mental note to take a breath and think about my answer before responding to any question, regardless of who asked it ... a client, opposing counsel, an acquaintance, or my husband. Eventually, that technique came back to haunt me when my husband would pick on me for talking too slowly. Now, I vary how long I think about a response based upon the audience. My husband mentored from the opposite direction.

As lawyers, we owe it to ourselves, our colleagues, and the general public to have mentors and to mentor others in our profession. But what does it mean to be a mentor?
What does a mentor look like?

According to the Cambridge Dictionary, a mentor is an

"experienced and trusted person
who gives another person advice and help,
especially related to work or school,
over a period of time."

Some of my greatest mentors were attorneys on the opposite side of cases. I began practicing law at the age of 28. Men still dominated the legal field, even though women comprised about 40% of my graduating class.

After graduating from law school, I moved back to my hometown of Wausau, Wisconsin. In Central Wisconsin, female attorneys probably comprised less than 25% of the legal community, and the further North you traveled, the fewer female attorneys you saw. The older male attorneys I encountered in Central and Northern Wisconsin left me with a generally poor impression. I regularly dealt with lawyers I describe as a bunch of chauvinistic old codgers. When younger female attorneys didn't stand up for themselves, these older attorneys would smell blood in the water and attack. Of course, they likely viewed their behavior as zealous advocacy.

However, being one of those women on the receiving end, I did not agree.

Perhaps it is my competitive nature, maybe it's how I was raised, but having anyone else, regardless of age or gender, try to bully me to get their way doesn't sit well with me. It didn't then either, so I stood firm and didn't let anyone push me around in a case. From my vantage point, I paid close attention to those I encountered. I selected the behaviors I wanted to emulate, and those I determined to avoid. All those attorneys unknowingly mentored me; some positively, some negatively.

My first legal job presented me with plenty of opportunities to stand up for myself. The senior attorney had a reputation of walking over associates and support staff until they quit. As a clerk following my first year of law school, I realized how little I knew to work in a law firm. But as much as he tried to intimidate me, it didn't work. Little did I know, I challenged him as much as he challenged me. At our firm Christmas party that year, Konrad's wife complimented me on sticking to my guns. She shared that every day that summer, Konrad would come home at night and say, "Mary, you wouldn't believe what Sarah said today" or "Mary, you wouldn't believe what Sarah did today." She laughed and told me to keep it up because people, especially women, did not typically stand up to Konrad— until me. I continued to do just that until I opened my firm about ten years later.

Lawyers generally want to help people.

As a profession, however, we're not very good about assisting each other, especially female attorneys helping other female attorneys. Aggressive, negative behavior does not paint a positive picture of the legal profession. It doesn't have to be this way. When we change our thoughts, we change the world. How we think affects how we interact with younger and older attorneys alike, with those with more experience, similar, and less. Imagine what will happen when we treat each other with a focus on helping rather than hindering, just like we treat our clients.

Younger lawyers need and usually appreciate guidance and understanding.

One of the very first files on my desk as a new lawyer involved a criminal complaint, though our firm did not handle criminal cases. One of our clients had two former employees who filed a complaint with the District Attorney alleging that the employer did not pay them overtime. The employer had a big problem: the employees had fabricated handwritten time cards to support their claim, which meant the employer had the burden to prove a negative to defend itself. After reading the file, I walked into Konrad's office and asked about it.

> "We don't do criminal work," I commented.
> "You do now," he responded.
> I asked what I needed to do.
> "Figure it out and do it."

That's exactly what I did. Trial by fire. What a way to mentor.

I encountered more mentoring on that file when I attended the initial appearance. I'd never been to a court appearance, much less a criminal initial appearance. When I arrived at the courtroom, I found a seat on one of the benches away from the rest of the defendants but didn't sit by the lawyers. The judge called all of the cases for defendants represented by lawyers first. When he finished, he started his speech with "now that everyone who is represented has been taken care of ..." and began to explain the process. I raised my hand. He acknowledged me and asked what I wanted. When I told him I was an attorney, he motioned me to go

78

to the podium in front of him. I had carefully noted what the attorneys before me did and said when approaching the judge. Our exchange went as follows:

Court: "What is your name?"
Me: "Sarah Rudolph, your Honor."
Court: "Who do you work for?"
Me: "Tuchscherer Law Firm."
Court: "Proceed."

The Judge looked down as if to tell me I had passed. The rest of the appearance went smoothly, comparable to the ones before me.

I learned a great lesson that day, namely that I can adequately learn how to represent a client in an unknown area of law. But I can certainly think of better ways to guide new lawyers! So, when assigning a project to a new lawyer, I prepare a delegation form outlining how we got to where we are, what we need to do, and list the steps to tackle the issue. I spend time with the lawyer discussing the process and answering questions. Before a court appearance, I suggest that lawyers observe similar proceedings at the courthouse. Young lawyers experience stage jitters before going to court, and those jitters diminish when they have some idea of what will happen.

So, how do you recognize a mentor when you see one?

What does the ideal mentor look like for you? What qualities do you have that make you a potential mentor for another person? When looking for a mentor, think about the qualities and skills that a person will possess. For example, do you want to hone your negotiation skills? Storytelling abilities? Litigation skills? Managerial prowess for your office?

Look for a person who, from your perspective, has mastered the skills you want to acquire or improve.

Remember that your ideal mentor will only be such until you have learned the lessons needed to take you to the next plateau, and you'll both move on. You'll reach your mentor's limits at some point, unless, like you, your mentor continues to grow. Most people eventually outgrow their mentors, which is as it should be. To improve continually, always be on the lookout for your next mentor.

To date, I have worked with three different business coaches. Each coach helped my business or me with the issues at hand.

When we first opened Ruffi Law Offices, I worked with a business coach to make sure the firm started with a strong foundation. With his guidance, we determined that Ruffi Law Offices was in the "peace of mind" business and identified our core principles. We likened our work to laying the foundation for a home. Without a strong foundation, we would have had an unstable building. The same rule applies to a law firm.

> *"A mentor is someone who allows you to see the hope inside yourself. A mentor is someone who allows you to know that no matter how dark the night, in the morning joy will come. A mentor is someone who allows you to see the higher part of yourself when sometimes it becomes hidden to your own view."*
>
> *Oprah Winfrey*

My second coach focused on systems to make the office run more smoothly and function as a business, not a high paying job. Under his guidance and with his encouragement, we worked to create systems, checklists, and forms for all aspects of our practice. Many of the pointers I picked up while working with him are incorporated into this book because they have become part of who I am.

My third coach helped me clarify my vision and goals and kept me on track to achieve those goals. She had a wealth of knowledge to share about personal improvement. Her mind contained a veritable library of book suggestions for life issues. She saved me a ton of research time on numerous topics by recommending the perfect book for the current situation.

In addition to business coaches, I have sought out particular mentors to assist me in skills and practice.

Areas of focus have included negotiation, trial preparation techniques, client development, team management, and recommendations for a variety of practice areas.

Ask yourself, "What do I need?" and "Who can fill that void?" Once you have completed your wish list, look for people who fit as many of your criteria as you can find. Be sure to ask others for suggestions too.

Ask for their help.

Live with their answer. Hopefully, they'll say yes; people are usually willing to come to your aide. However, if a prospective mentor says no, it may mean that they simply do not have time, do not feel qualified, or they are not the right person to be your mentor at that time. Keep looking for the perfect fit. The correct mentor will appear when you are ready. As Buddha Siddhartha Guatama Shakyamuni said, "When the student is ready, the teacher will appear."

When you find a mentor, make sure you fit the role of a mentee.

Are you **coachable**? Are you **ready and willing to learn**? Will you **accept** and **incorporate** the mentor's suggestions even if you don't agree? Are you respectful of the mentor's time? Are you respectful of the mentor's trust? As with everything in life, you get out what you put into the situation. Give 150%, so you receive what you deserve, and your mentor does too. When your mentor gives you a suggestion, try it, or the mentor may lose interest in mentoring you.

By being a good mentee, you will receive numerous benefits. You can obtain the most out of a mentoring relationship. You will expand your professional network. You can receive advice on how to achieve career goals. You will be in a position to establish allies and find opportunities.

The day will eventually come for your mentorship to conclude. Expect some awkwardness in this part of the process but resolve to rise above it and finish with dignity. Honor your mentor in a way they will appreciate. Graciously express your gratitude as the mentoring relationship concludes.

Then, when no one is looking, page ahead in your planner and leave yourself a note to invite your now-former mentor to coffee or lunch. They invested in you and will enjoy hearing how you're using what they taught you. As President John F. Kennedy once said, "We must find time to stop and thank the people who make a difference in our lives."

When an aspiring lawyer wants to learn from you all about this or that, pause to remember how much your mentors taught you. Smile and agree to discuss the possibility. You don't have to make it easy for them – but do make it possible. You've had mentors. It's time to be a mentor.

Whether you are the mentor or the mentee, treat the other person with respect, dignity, openness, understanding, and professionalism. Think about the type of person you want to be — your favorite.

"My favorite mentor unleashed my passions, channeled my energy, guided my growth, and encouraged my success."

Anna Letitia Cook
Director, WomenUP Ltd.

Take Control of Your Life

"It's not the load that breaks you down, it's the way you carry it."
Lou Holtz

Have you felt overwhelming stress due to your job? Endured tension headaches? How often do you arrive at home at night, with no patience - you've got too much on your mind?!

You need to take control of things and get some relief!

Think of managing your life using the Stress RELIEF system. A friend and I came up with this a while back.

RELIEF stands for:

Realization
Enlistment
Love
Individuality
Environment
Fulfillment

Realization. Realize that life consists of more than working all the time. Realize that you and your family come first. After all, it's by taking good care of ourselves that we are best suited to care for our loved ones and clients.

I remember as a young lawyer working at a small firm, I was the lead attorney in a big non-compete case in Federal Court (more work than State Court) against a big firm from Madison, Wisconsin. Well, they decided to paper us to death in an attempt to win the case. In the middle of all this, Dwight, my boyfriend now husband, decided to throw me a surprise birthday party one Friday night.

85

He planned everything, including inviting all my co-workers and my parents. I had been working every day until 8:00 pm or later. One Friday night, everyone in the office waited for me to finish a phone call to tell me to have a good weekend, which was not the norm. Usually, if I was on a phone call, they just waved and left the office or simply left without a good-bye. Pre-occupied, I didn't even realize how different things were that night. Dwight called me several times to make sure that I was going to be on time for the birthday party "for a friend's son." He even asked me to pick up a couple of things on my way.

When I arrived at the hotel for the party, I saw my parents' car in the parking lot. I thought, "How could they go out to dinner while my sister is in town and not invite us? How irritating!" Entering the hotel, I saw Dwight standing on the far side of the swimming pool holding a baby. I walked toward him, down the hallway to the pool, trying with every step to figure out, "Whose baby?" Then I saw one of the attorneys from the firm and realized, "This party is for me — and that baby is our godson!" I couldn't believe it! At that moment, I realized that my world existed solely within the four walls of my firm —my office— and that had to change. Now.

I wish I could tell you that was the only time I answered a wakeup call about how my law practice consumed my life. "With age comes wisdom." Right? Not solely with age, I must say. Wisdom sometimes comes in the form of people around you complaining that you're distant or pre-occupied, even when you're physically present.

The expression "wherever you are, be all there" applies. But it takes self-discipline to put your life ahead of your career.

Enlistment. You don't have to be Wonder Woman, doing everything yourself. Enlist the help of those around you; your significant other, your children, friends, colleagues, family, employees, even your clients. People generally want to help others, and sometimes the best thing to do is ask for help. Remember the adage, "ask, and you shall receive"? It is amazing what happens when we open ourselves up, be a little vulnerable, and ask for help.

Help sometimes comes from the most unlikely sources. When my husband and I decided to open our own firm, help came our way from many places and a variety of people. Dwight spent many hours scouring our hometown for the right space for Ruffi Law Offices, S.C. to call home. During a meeting with a banker, who was also a client, I asked if the bank would loan us money to open a firm. He responded that he would help with whatever we needed. He commented that an older attorney had joined another firm on his road to retirement and his office was available. I mentioned that everything needed to be strictly confidential because if my partners found out about our plans, I would be fired. He promised to keep our secret. And he did! Eight years or so after opening our firm, at this gentleman's funeral, we told his wife how much he helped us when we first started out. She had no idea. He'd kept our secret — even from his wife.

My husband called the attorney referred by the banker. His space was available, so Dwight checked it out. Because he wanted to see us succeed, he agreed to lease the space to us at a low rental rate. (We rented from him for seven years until we purchased our own building.)

While we remodeled the space before moving in, Dwight and I took shifts caring for our two young boys. I worked at my lawyer job while Dwight watched the boys during the day. Dwight remodeled while I watched the boys each night. My parents watched the boys on weekends so we could both work on the remodel. We enlisted the help of close friends who helped rip up carpeting, remove wallpaper, build a wall, paint, and clean.

When it was time to open the doors, friends loaned us a laser printer. Another law firm offered to let me use their library and a set of Wisconsin Statutes until I had my library set up. Still another firm referred potential clients to me and kept my phone number by the receptionist's desk.

Even clients helped us get off to a good start. One person approached me at a networking event the week after we opened, told me that he wanted to work with me, but wouldn't work with my old partners. He soon transitioned, and his business became one of my biggest clients.

Sometimes, all it takes is a little help from some friends. (Are you humming the Beatles song now? Good.) Don't be too proud to ask for a little help. You never know who knows the perfect person to help you out and at what point they will arrive.

Love. Sometimes we get so busy and wrapped up in our jobs that we forget to enjoy the simpler things in life. Like love. Oh, it gets complicated occasionally, but for the most part, love is rather simple and straightforward. It has many rewarding facets.

As a woman lawyer, you need to keep three aspects of love in good healthy balance:
   your **profession**,
   your **relationships**,
   and **yourself**.

Love the profession of law. Never forget why you entered the legal profession. Choose every day to love what you do, where you do it, and for whom you do it– your clients.

Initially, I became a lawyer because, as a business owner, I didn't want to need a lawyer continually. I later realized that the practice of law is actually my purpose in life. I love helping my clients figure out their problems. After the birth of my second son, I ventured out on my own because while I loved my clients, I hated where I practiced law. Now, I love many of my clients, and I love where I practice.

Love your relationships – Who in your life do you love? Do you make time to share your love? Yes, that's make time. You must intentionally make the time –set it aside– to spend time with the special people in your life.

I incorporate my family into my firm by design, because I love them. I'm enjoying the best of both worlds. The men who mean everything to me know many of my clients, who, in turn, have watched my boys grow up over the years. My husband and boys frequent the office. We network as a family.

Your setting differs from mine, but deliberately make the time to grow and maintain relationships with those you love. Make sure your staff knows your family schedule. For example, when one of my sons has a soccer game, swimming match, or concert, I'll be there, not at the office, regardless of the time of day.

Love yourself. How you speak to yourself, treat yourself, even pamper yourself, affects how you come across to clients, the business community, and in the courtroom. As women, we typically worry about taking care of everyone else before thinking of ourselves. The harsh reality is, if we neglect ourselves, eventually, we will not be able to take care of anyone else either.

Love takes time. Remember to take the time to find and feel love. Love yourself and those around you unconditionally. Take time each day to focus on life's blessings. Periodically treat yourself to something you really enjoy. Maybe it's weekend excursions with friends. Perhaps hiking, scrapbooking, traveling, meditating, shopping, music, painting, reading? Skydiving, maybe? Whatever it is, mark time out in your calendar and do it.

For example, I love to work on scrapbooks for my boys. While I'm scrapbooking, I think about them, replay the memories going into those volumes, and I smile. Two or three times a year, I escape the office grind for a ladies scrapbooking weekend retreat at a nearby hotel. While it's a Mom weekend, Dwight usually brings the boys by the hotel once or twice to see me (for a minute) and relax by the pool (for a couple of hours).

Some of the women who have attended these retreats have watched my boys grow up and enjoy seeing how they've grown. They share my passion for documenting moments in time through pictures and designs. Some are clients I serve, some I'll maybe serve someday.

Love yourself and know that you have what it takes to succeed. Love others and know that you have what it takes to care for them. Build times into your life where you can enjoy the things you love. You'll be better for it.

Individuality. We are all individuals, but sometimes we forget to be ourselves. Do you know the individual characteristics that make you who you are? Those characteristics help clients seek you out among others in your field. Learn to take advantage of your attributes. While we selected a career in a male-dominated world, we can still be ourselves. Embrace your feminine energy and the motto: "I am woman, hear me roar!"

A couple of years ago, I went to a women's weekend retreat. In one session, the presenter discussed masculine and feminine energy. She asked us each to decide if we are more masculine or more feminine. Imagine my surprise when she picked me to prove a point. Commenting that I come across as quite masculine, she asked me what color underwear I was wearing. I doubt anyone in the room expected me to answer "leopard print"! She then pointed out how my entire demeanor changed when I responded, and that deep down I was quite feminine. At that moment, I made a conscious decision to allow my feminine energy out more often! And why not? Our feminine energy highlights compassion, love, nurturing, and empathy more so than masculine energy. By using my feminine energy, I have been able to soften clients, opposing counsel, and opposing parties, helping move toward a resolution of the issue on the table.

When we forget to be ourselves, we tend to lose ourselves. So be authentic. No circumstance, case, or situation will ever be perfect. Neither will you. But you can know your individuality and thrive — without perfection. Take the chance and let your individuality show. This is not to say that you have to be boisterous and a fool, but rather a person accepting of all.

One more thing. If you want to be an individual accepted for "YOU," it's best to accept others. Think highly, because you are what you think about. Set your standards accordingly. Now let the real you show through. That's authentic individuality.

Environment. Whether you own your firm or work for someone, you can design your environment to suit your character and personality. Design your office —whether a small cubicle or a large corner office— to be a highly productive zone that reflects your strengths and personality. It may be as simple as what you use as a screen saver on your computer, your calendar, items on your desk, or around your office. Shape your environment with pictures, motivational expressions, color scheme, kids' artwork, your choice of coffee or tea mug, even your favorite music playing in the background. Design your environment, so your work is a place you enjoy.

Remember my mentioning when a new client walked into our office one day and commented, "I feel like I am walking into a friend's home"? While those words pleasantly surprised me, they also confirmed that we're achieving one of our goals: creating a warm, comfortable, and welcoming environment. Our walls feature paintings done by my husband and one of the boys, quotes, even a picture of Jesus. I display pictures of my boys in my office and conference room. The sofa and chairs in my office are comfortable and relaxing.

Knick-knacks from a client embellish my bookcase; an old jar of smelling salts and an antique desk bell. My office feels like a home away from home, which makes perfect sense, after all. Yours might as well suit you too.

Fulfillment. Fulfillment is not about being the best in your field. It is about being able to measure and keep the balance in everyday life. Ask yourself, "Am I living my purpose? Am I fulfilled? Am I making my dreams come true? Am I doing what I want to do? What's working? What's not working? Am I happy?" Life is dynamic. So when something stops working for you, feel free to unplug, change or delete it.

You need both long-range perspective and day-to-day assessment to monitor how you're doing. When life gets busy, as it's prone to do, we forget to look around and express gratitude for all the blessings in life. Including three things in your daily routine will help you maintain your fulfillment and gratitude balance:

Begin your day with something inspiring.

End each day reflecting on the good things that happened during the day. Ask yourself, "What good things happened today? What am I grateful for today?"

Give thanks for the things and relationships you enjoy.

A dream is a dream.
When you assign a deadline, it becomes a goal.

Decide what you want to do and by when then create your plan, considering professional and personal ambitions. Set annual, monthly, weekly, and daily goals and objectives. Write them down, yes, but more importantly, review them daily with a critical eye. Have analysis checkpoints to ask yourself why you reached a specific goal — or missed it.

Make sure you take care of all areas of your life, including time for your health and well-being. Remember, if you feel empty, you'll deliver empty to your family, your clients, and everyone you meet. That's not what you want, so take the time —ahead of time— to prevent it from happening.

Here's how it worked for the woman who designed our Woman Warrior Lawyer logo. During our conversation one day, she told me about when she and her husband decided it was time for her to quit her job so she could care for their family. They agreed that she would offer daycare until her graphic design business took off. She posted on Facebook and soon was watching a baby the same age as her daughter. Two years later, those girls are the best of friends, and she has all sorts of graphic design jobs coming in, via phone and internet. As she described how it all happened, I could hear the excitement of adventure anticipating what is going to happen to her business next. Isn't that part of what life is all about? Take the chances that keep your heart beating with adventure and happiness. Sometimes it'll even take your breath away.

We master certain skills or methods in life to help us at certain times. As we grow, we leave things behind. Our gifts we intentionally develop and keep sharp. Atrophy results in that sense of dread; "I'm unfulfilled." That's not what you want.

Remember being told as a child that you can do whatever you set your mind to do? Do you still believe that? I hope so! If not, rekindle that inner voice and direction. Decide —or decide again— what you want out of life and go after it.

If you want more from your life or career, define what your "more" looks like and pursue it.

It's not too late to accomplish what you set your mind to do. Focus on what you want in life, remembering that where focus goes, energy flows.

Create a clear picture of how you want your life to be. Once you have that picture, visualize it. What does it look like? What do you see? What do you hear? What do you smell? Make your picture real in your mind's eye and create goals from your picture. Since our minds can't distinguish between real and imaginary, make your dream real in your mind. Then, your subconscious can kick in and help you find a way to make your dream a reality.

"If you can dream it, you can do it."
                          Walt Disney

Now, go do it. Live your dream.

Afterword

As women, we are conditioned to put everyone else before ourselves: Our spouses. Our kids. Our clients. Our employees. Fortunately, we have the ability and the right to change our priorities. It's OK to release our inner warrior and take the lead!

Katharine Graham grew up in the newspaper business. Her father led The Washington Post as its Editor. Eventually, Katharine married Phil, who worked at The Washington Post while she entertained their elite circle of friends which included high ranking government officials and two U.S. presidents. Her father named Phil as the new Editor when he retired, and Katharine had no problem with her husband taking control of her family's business; it fit the times.

But in August of 1963, Phil took his own life. Overnight, Katharine became the Editor of The Washington Post. She relied on a close circle of her husband's friends rather than follow her internal compass. She had a seat at the board meeting table, but not a voice.

At the advice of her board and bankers, she decided to take The Washington Post public. The board's prospectus included a provision enabling the bankers to withdraw their investment if a "catastrophic event" occurred within seven days of the offering. Katharine focused on this provision.

About this time, The New York Times began running a series of articles about a cover-up by the U.S. government over the Vietnam conflict that spanned four presidencies.

The government sued The New York Times and obtained an injunction against it and its agents, which arguably included the source of information on the stories. The lawsuit gave The Washington Post an opportunity to catch up with The New York Times.

The Washington Post acquired a copy of the report that The New York Times likely used for its articles, and within hours, had a story ready to run. The news staff demanded that Katharine take a stand with the First Amendment and run the story. Her advisors and attorneys, on the other hand, insisted that she follow the safe route and wait. Katharine found herself in a stand-off. They held the presses, but to have the papers ready for the morning drop, they needed to start by midnight.

Reaching deep inside, Katharine seized control of her true self and found her voice. She informed the men standing in her home that The Washington Post did not belong to her father or her husband. It was HER company. Though she could be imprisoned for contempt, The Washington Post would publish the Vietnam articles.

At 12:15 a.m., the presses rolled.

Newspapers all over the country stood with her and published stories about Vietnam and The Washington Post's fight with the Nixon Administration. No longer just Phil's wife, she became a leader in the newspaper industry.

You, like Katharine, chose a male-dominated career. While you may need to work extra hard to prove your skills, you're the one designing your practice and building your team – a strong team. You control your schedule, deciding what to delegate, and how. You decide who you'll mentor. You set the pace for your firm's networking style, the one in charge. You'll have countless opportunities as a woman to diffuse and navigate difficult, stressful situations.

When you honor yourself, your inner voice, and your strength, amazing things happen. Choose your own path, not the one your parents, friends, or society wish you to walk.

Today is your day. Seize it.

Index

Notes

Notes

Notes

Made in the USA
San Bernardino, CA
23 February 2020